MONEY RULES
Your Choices, Your Future.

Money Rules for Women

THE PROVEN SECRET SYSTEM TO MASTER YOUR MONEY AND ACHIEVE FINANCIAL CERTAINTY

NOBBY KLEINMAN

Money Rules

First edition 2023

National Library of Australia
Cataloguing-in-Publication entry:

Kleinman, Nobby
Money Rules: The Proven Secret System To Master Your Money And Achieve Financial Certainty/ **Nobby Kleinman**

1st Ed
ISBN 978-0-9807107-4-8

Women - Finance, PersonalFinance Saving and Wealth Creation

For bulk copies of this book or general information on other products and services by Nobby Kleinman, contact ask@Money Rules.com.au

ISBN: Paperback 978-0-9807107-4-8
ISBN: eBook 978-0-9807107-5-5

Printed in Australia.

Kleinman, Nobby. Money Rules: The Proven Secret System To Master Your Money And Achieve Financial Certainty

Kindle Edition.

TABLE OF CONTENTS

ACKNOWLEDGEMENTS

After spending 20 years of my life working as a financial adviser, I found it impossible to let go of my passion for helping people with their finances. A common concern, especially among women, happened when they were seeking advice on managing their money. Instead of genuine financial guidance, they often encountered a sea of financial products. They had no one to turn to for advice on managing their money. It was this observation that made me realize the significant gap in the financial advice services that needed addressing.

This journey traces back to my days as a financial adviser when women frequently posed one specific question which I address later in this book. This one single, simple question, would play a pivotal role in my return to financial advice without the product-centric approach and without being aligned with the insurance companies or banks.

I am immensely grateful to those who asked that question. It became the driving force behind the creation of a practical, push-button solution. Men have described it as a 'no-brainer.' Women praised its simplicity of understanding and use.

Through this process, I've gained profound insights into the strength and resilience of women and the sacrifices they make in life. Engaging in this project over the years since 2008 I discovered that the deeper you delve, the more challenging it becomes. Our world is in turmoil and seems to be sinking ever deeper without real solutions for most. Many face ruined lives, homelessness, fear, anxiety, and uncertainty. Financial futures are not guaranteed and many are living a life less than they should or deserve.

Today, I extend my heartfelt acknowledgment to those women whose questions inspired me to build something truly unique—a platform that empowers countless others to master their money and create future wealth, security and certainty. The feedback I've received reflects a renewed perspective on life management, enabling individuals to plan for their futures well in advance and take back control.

I'm extremely proud to have developed this program and to have had the privilege of working with so many remarkable women. It wouldn't have been possible without their questions. To them and to every woman I've had the honour to collaborate with, I wholeheartedly say 'THANK YOU!"

And for the men reading this—rest assured, it's equally effective for you. It even comes with instructions.

MONEY RULES

Your Choices. Your Future.

AN OFFER SO GOOD

Get this Results In Advance eBook & report

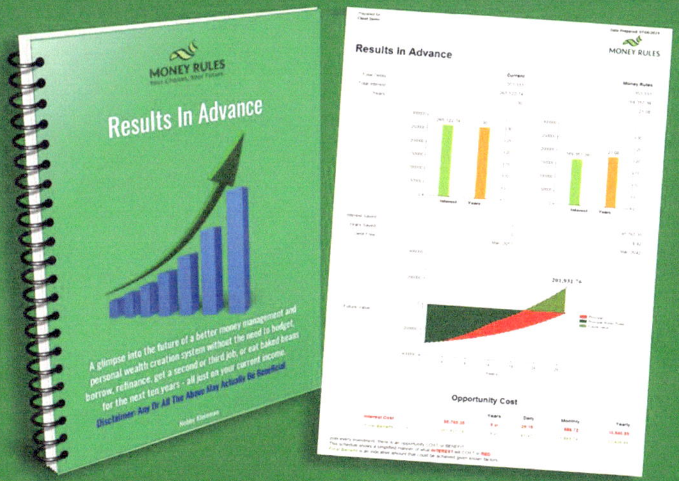

Your Future Depends On It

INTRODUCTION

In a world where the strings of power are pulled by big money, vast organizations, and formidable government entities, we often find ourselves navigating a maze of influence and control. From the moment we step into this complex landscape, we are bombarded with messages telling us what is best for us, how we should live our lives, and what we should aspire to become. It's a world where the pursuit of our dreams can easily be overshadowed by the agendas of those who sit at the apex of society.

But what if there was a way to break free from these invisible chains, reclaim our autonomy and forge a path uniquely our own? What if financial independence held the key to unlocking the life we've always yearned for, one free from the dictates of others and driven by our aspirations?

The journey to true financial liberation is an odyssey worth embarking upon. In these pages, we will unravel the enigma of wealth, debt, and the power it wields over us. We will explore the profound impact of financial control, particularly for those ensnared by the clutches of debt.

But fear not, for the answers you seek are within reach, and they are refreshingly uncomplicated. This book is your guiding light, your map to navigating the treacherous waters of finance without resorting to the hype of manifestation or relying solely on hope, prayer, and wishful thinking.

Join me on a transformative journey, where you will learn how to master your money, vanquish your debts, and craft a future bursting with wealth, all within the confines of your current income. Remember, everything is relative. Your income shapes your lifestyle, but it need not be the sole determinant of your dreams. Others have shattered these limitations and soared to unprecedented heights.

The question is, why not you?

Is this what you are seeking?

Is this your holy grail?

Prepare to break free from the shackles of financial control and embark on a journey toward the life of your dreams. This book is your invitation to uncover the secrets of financial independence, seize your destiny, and take control of your life. Your path to a brighter future begins here.

Let's go!

"ACRES OF DIAMONDS"
(abbreviated) by Russell H. Conwell

Once, there was a farmer who lived in Africa and owned a modest plot of land. He constantly dreamed of discovering diamonds, as he believed that owning a diamond mine would bring him immense wealth. Dissatisfied with his life and convinced that he could only find riches elsewhere, he sold his farm and left in search of diamonds.

Years passed, and the man travelled the world in pursuit of his dream but found no diamonds. Eventually, he exhausted his savings and became destitute. In a state of despair, he took his own life.

Meanwhile, back at the farm he had sold, the new owner was ploughing the fields when he discovered something shiny in the earth. It turned out to be a large diamond, and as he continued to dig, he found more and more diamonds in abundance.

The farm the first man had owned was situated on a massive diamond deposit, one of the world's richest sources of diamonds. However, he never knew it because he had abandoned his land in search of wealth elsewhere.

This story teaches us that success and opportunities are often right in front of us if we pay attention. Instead of searching far and wide for riches, we can find valuable opportunities in our everyday lives, jobs, and surroundings.

I'll introduce you to a meticulously crafted program that can help you discover your hidden treasures and potential if you're interested. These principles and the program have the power to transform your life and create financial certainty.

Within the following pages, you'll explore a program that can unlock the wealth you've been seeking, right within your own life. It's an exciting journey filled with promise and untapped potential. As we delve deeper, you'll gain the ability to secure your financial future in your way. If life hasn't taken you where you expected, then let's embark on a journey together to reach the destination you truly desire.

Never before in the history of humanity has this information been of greater need.

You have in your control the key to your financial future.

WILL I HAVE ENOUGH?

This seemingly simple yet profoundly impactful question plagues the minds of many on their journey to retirement. The path to financial security is strewn with the remnants of dreams and aspirations, left behind by those who walked it before us. Why did they falter? What crucial piece of the puzzle eluded them?

The journey begins with a dream—a vision of a better life for ourselves, our children, and our grandchildren. Yet, along the way, we encounter obstacles and setbacks. We blame ourselves for not being smart enough, and not working hard enough, and we make sacrifices we never thought we would.

Less than 10% of the population go to see a financial adviser because they don't think they have enough money. Most financial advisers are looking to work with HNW clients (High Net Worth) and advised clients generally end up better financially.

That means 90% of the population never gets to see a financial adviser.

More than 75% of the population is living from one pay to the next.

Whenever you ask financial experts, they recommend a minimum savings of three to six months' worth of expenses for emergencies. Yet 42% of most households have less than $1,000 in savings, and 10% have none at all. Few people are able to scrape together $400 in the event of an immediate emergency.

Around 50% or more people retiring do so still carrying personal and mortgage debt.

When I asked them why, they told me they were too busy working to pay the bills!

Women are more at risk than men for a variety of reasons.

But what if I told you it didn't have to be this way?

What if you could have the critical information that has been missing all along?

That missing piece of knowledge that is widely available but never acknowledged!

Most people are unaware that their financial decisions are built on flawed concepts, leading to a journey riddled with uncertainty, stress, and unnecessary risk. They follow the same broken methods as those who came before them, spending the prime years of their lives chasing an elusive dream. Get an education, get a job, buy a car, get married, buy a house, have a family, work until retirement, rest in peace.

Tragically, this cycle repeats itself. The next generation embarks on the same path only to discover decades later that their dreams too are buried beneath the weight of financial insecurity.

Financial planning itself isn't the answer because it often focuses more on long-term investments and less on the immediate financial security and lifestyle needs that individuals require. What everyone wants is financial certainty and to be able to see it and evaluate it with their own eyes, minds and hearts.

That's why most individuals couldn't confidently answer the question, 'Will I have enough?'—until the introduction of Money Rules.

Money Rules is a system based on a proven mathematical formula that focuses on money management, debt elimination, and wealth creation. While others chase elusive goals, we focus on clarity, empowerment, and results. Money Rules distils the complexities into one intelligent system. Just one hour per month can yield results in a matter of weeks. It's a journey that brings you closer to financial freedom—faster, safer, with unwavering certainty and significantly less stress.

Imagine someone handing you the key to your future. It's your shortcut to success.

It empowers individuals to take control of their financial destiny, coping with the daily grind in pursuit of an exact financial freedom date. Money Rules provides absolute predictability and moves individuals from fear to empowerment, from chaos to clarity, confidence and certainty, from stress to peace of mind, and all with a simple systematic approach. This is easier to do than not!

Welcome to Money Rules—a transformative journey that redefines the way we think about financial security and paves the way to a brighter, more certain future.

Women would always ask me for the secret of how to manage their money. I told them, but they didn't believe it could be that simple.

What they really wanted - *really needed* - was a push-button solution!

So I built the system to help them.

I'll share with you 'The Proven Secret System To Master Your Money And Achieve Financial Certainty' if that's what you really want!

Nobby Kleinman Adv Dip FS (FP)

WELCOME TO YOUR FINANCIAL FREEDOM

Welcome to the journey towards achieving true financial freedom. In these pages, you will embark on a transformative adventure that will forever change the way you think about money, wealth, and your financial potential.

Whether you've been grappling with financial stress, seeking to take control of your destiny, or simply looking to secure a brighter financial future, you've come to the right place.

Together, we will explore the path to financial empowerment, and by the end of this journey, you'll be equipped with the tools, knowledge, and confidence needed to shape your financial destiny.

Throughout more than two decades in the world of financial services, I've had the privilege of working with thousands of individuals from all walks of life. I've witnessed their challenges, aspirations, and dreams. I've seen firsthand the hurdles that can hinder financial growth and the remarkable transformations that can occur when one takes control of their financial life.

Now, I'm here to share those insights with you. This book is not just a compilation of financial advice; it's your personalized guide to unlocking the door to financial freedom.

I understand that financial matters can sometimes be overwhelming, intimidating, or even shrouded in mystery. But let me assure you, it doesn't have to be that way. My mission is to demystify the world of personal finance and provide you with a clear, actionable roadmap to financial independence.

By the time you finish reading these pages, you'll not only have a deeper understanding of your financial situation but also the confidence to make informed decisions that can lead to a life of security and abundance.

So, welcome to this empowering journey. Open your mind and your heart to the possibilities that lie ahead.

As we explore the principles of Money Rules and embrace a new way of thinking, remember that financial freedom is not a distant dream but a tangible goal within your reach.

The power to transform your financial life starts here, and I'm honoured to be your guide on this path to prosperity.

"In the middle of every difficulty lies opportunity."
- Albert Einstein

CHAPTER 1

WOMEN AND THEIR FINANCIAL JOURNEY

The Unique Challenges Women Face

The financial journey of women is a remarkable and complex narrative filled with unique challenges and triumphs. Throughout history, women have navigated a financial landscape shaped by societal norms, gender biases, and evolving roles. Understanding these distinctive challenges is the first step toward empowering women to take control of their financial destinies. The intricacies of these challenges offer insights into how women have overcome them.

One of the most significant challenges women face is the gender pay gap. Despite progress in recent years, women still earn less than their male counterparts for the same work. This disparity not only affects women's immediate financial well-being but also impacts their ability to save, invest, and plan for the future. Additionally, women often bear the responsibilities of caregiving, which can lead to career interruptions and reduced earning potential.

The unique challenges women face extend beyond income disparities. They also include a greater likelihood of facing major life transitions such as divorce, widowhood, or caring for aging parents. These transitions can bring emotional and financial upheaval, making it crucial for women to have the knowledge and resources to navigate these changes successfully.

Understanding and acknowledging these challenges is essential, but it's equally vital to recognize that women possess incredible resilience, resourcefulness, and determination. By addressing these unique hurdles head-on and seeking empowerment, women can rewrite their financial stories and pave the way for a brighter, more secure future.

Empowering Women for Financial Independence

Empowering women for financial independence is not just a goal; it's a necessity. It's about recognizing the immense potential and strength that women bring to the financial world. It's acknowledging that women are leaders, decision-makers, and change-makers in their own right. Here, we'll explore the pathways to empowerment and the tools that can help women achieve financial independence.

Financial empowerment begins with knowledge. It's about understanding the financial landscape, from money management and investing to debt management and retirement planning. Women have a right to this knowledge, and they should actively seek it. Financial literacy is not a luxury but a powerful tool for shaping one's financial destiny. There's so much more to be said and done in this area alone.

In addition to knowledge, empowerment is also about building a supportive network. Women can benefit greatly from connecting with mentors, peers, and advisors who understand their unique financial challenges and aspirations. These relationships can provide guidance, inspiration, and a sense of community on the journey toward financial independence.

Empowerment is not a one-size-fits-all concept. It's about tailoring financial strategies to align with individual goals and circumstances. Whether it's pursuing entrepreneurship, investing in education, or building a robust financial plan, women have the capacity to chart their own paths to success. Empowerment is about choice, and every financial decision is a step toward greater independence.

Taking Control of Your Financial Destiny

Taking control of your financial destiny is both a mindset and a series of actions. It's the realization that your financial future is not determined by external factors alone but by the choices you make today. This section delves into the principles and strategies that can help women seize control of their financial destinies and shape the lives they desire.

At the core of taking control is setting clear financial goals. Whether it's achieving homeownership, securing a comfortable retirement, or starting a business, defining your aspirations is the first step. Your goals become the roadmap guiding your financial decisions and actions.

Financial planning and organization are key tools in taking control. Creating a plan, managing debt, saving consistently, and reinvesting are foundational steps. These actions provide the financial stability and security necessary to pursue your dreams with confidence.

Whether you engage with Money Rules or any other program, taking control of your financial future begins with the act of doing something. That means you need to know your numbers. And in order to do that will require some form of calculation, be it pen and paper, spreadsheets or a software program.

Here are some real-life stories of women, and men, who have taken control of their financial destinies after going through the Results In Advance process. Their experiences illustrate the power of determination, resilience, and informed decision-making. As you'll see, their journey towards financial independence is beyond anything they could conceive possible when they first started. As you read these results, consider how they resonate with your own financial aspirations.

	Recovered	**Saved**
Heather	12.42 years in lost time	$112,638 in wasted interest
Mario	18.42 years in lost time	$210,150 in wasted interest
Roger	22.17 years in lost time	£ 53,034 in wasted interest
Joanne	10.08 years in lost time	$2,397,686 in wasted interest
Cherie	15.5 years in lost time	$152,635 in wasted interest
Lynda	8.75 years in lost time	$ 80,396 in wasted interest
Krista	13.83 years in lost time	$ 82,878 in wasted interest
James	14.00 years in lost time	$201,524 in wasted interest

Taking control of your financial destiny is not just a possibility; it's a reality within reach. By embracing the unique challenges, seeking empowerment, and making intentional choices, you can break free from the constraints of financial uncertainty and step boldly into a future filled with independence and fulfilment

This process is more straightforward than you might imagine. You possess all the necessary information, and if not, it's readily available for the asking. The task of entering your details will require just a brief time investment, around 20 to 30 minutes. Once completed, you'll embark on a transformative journey, gaining fresh insights into your present and future financial landscape. You could also achieve results like those above.

If you're eager to get started – and we hope you are – head over to https://moneyrules.com.au/ria

There, you'll find a video that will guide you through the initial steps. Follow the recommendations, enter your details, and set yourself on the path to financial empowerment.

However, a word of caution. Taking this step is a significant commitment to change your financial future, and your trust in this process is considered seriously. I encourage you to proceed only if you are genuinely ready for this transformation, prepared to embrace change now, and committed to reshaping your financial destiny. Your journey to financial freedom starts with a single step, and it's a journey I'm excited to take with you.

"The best investment you can make is in yourself."

- Warren Buffett

CHAPTER 2

THE POWER OF FINANCIAL EMPOWERMENT

Understanding Your Financial Landscape

Understanding your financial landscape is the first step on your journey to financial empowerment. It's like embarking on a road trip with a reliable map in hand. Imagine you're setting out on an adventure to explore uncharted territories. Your financial landscape is your starting point, the place where you are today. It's essential to have a clear picture of where you stand, your assets, debts, income, and expenses. Only when you understand your current financial situation can you plan your route toward financial freedom effectively. It's about knowing your numbers.

Throughout my career, I've witnessed countless individuals who, despite their best intentions, struggled because they didn't fully grasp their financial landscape. They'd often attempt to navigate without a clear map, leading to financial stress and uncertainty. But you're different. By diving into this chapter, you're already demonstrating your commitment to taking control of your financial destiny. You're ready to shine a light on your financial landscape, uncovering both the challenges and opportunities that lie ahead.

A common thread I found, was that many individuals spent more time planning their annual holidays than they did planning for their future or retirement. They lived in the day and figured that tomorrow would take care of itself. They still had plenty of time!

This section will guide you through the process of assessing your financial landscape with simplicity and clarity. We'll explore how to create a comprehensive financial snapshot (Results In Advance) that captures the current critical elements of your financial life.

You'll discover the power of tracking your income, understanding your debts and expenses, and evaluating your spending. By the end, you'll have a solid foundation, a financial compass, that will enable you to make informed decisions and set a clear direction for your financial journey.

Sure, you've heard this all before and probably thought it was too hard.

When I was being asked by clients for help in managing their money, I'd give them my standard financial adviser response, 'Spend less than you earn and pay the highest interest debt first."

They would look at me waiting for more. "Surely it can't be that simple" is what they said. "There must be more to it than that," and that I must be withholding some *secret adviser knowledge* that I wasn't sharing with them!

Managing your money isn't rocket science! It's actually easier than you might think. And, **it's easier to do than not!** Within your mind, you probably already know this but don't believe it.

Planning for the annual holidays is no different. It's like boiling a kettle of water. The idea springs to mind and goes from cold to hot. You don't just go on holiday. You start meticulously planning weeks, months and sometimes even years before that actual event.

When you've decided on the destination, you'll decide how long the holiday will be, the accommodation type, the travel arrangements, the events you'll participate in, meals, shopping, entertainment, relaxation, spending, and finally the return agenda.

You'll choose the time of year to travel, necessary clothing and baggage allowances, important paperwork to carry, any medical arrangements and so on. I'm sure you can think of many more items to add to this list. Let's face it, who doesn't enjoy preparing and planning for a holiday?

Well, it's no different for planning a lifestyle in retirement. Nobody goes on holiday when they are broke, and retirement should be no different.

Many more people are arriving asset-rich and cash-poor at retirement is a growing issue around the world affecting more people every year, which means that eventually, they are going to rely on the government for social security.

The sad fact is that poverty is not a solution that most people who are living in it are happy with. Given their time again, most would be more active in their preparation. Many people do feel they are entitled to a government pension after all the years of tax contributions and they have to accept responsibility for their decisions.

I'm sure that's a prospect you are not looking forward to because you're reading this to get ahead financially. Let's work on that.

When you know your numbers you can start to plan for your future. Just like any financial management program or system, you need to have an understanding of your cash flow. It is simply about money in and money out.

When you start with Money Rules, you will be asked to provide incomes, expenses and debts. You will also be providing some other details such as the starting date which is normally the date you enter the information and the date you expect that item to stop.

There's nothing hard in that!

Let's consider a salary. The income is generally received on a regular basis and is likely to stop on the date that employment ceases. Quite often, that could coincide with retirement, so we have a good idea of the future date which might be age 65. The same applies to other incomes and expenses. Considering a child's education, this might stop at a certain age when the child expects to leave schooling and perhaps start working.

One common question from self-employed is that their income can go up and down like a yo-yo and without certainty. And yet they have managed to survive the past 12 months on that very same premise, never knowing if they would have enough pay expenses and overheads. Yet they managed.

So the answer is simply to take the previous 12 months to get a monthly average income. The other way is to use the actual monthly incomes from the last 12 months and enter those going forward. Then replace them with real-time incomes each month going forward.

When you look at fixed-term debts such as car or personal loans, they have a time period when they will end. Once this information has been entered, believe it or not, the hardest part is already over. It really is just that simple!

Remember, understanding your financial landscape is not about judgment or blame. It's about empowerment. Knowledge is power. The insights you gain here will be the tools you need to move forward with confidence, knowing that you have a deep understanding of your starting point. With this knowledge, you can set realistic goals, make informed choices, and ultimately navigate your way to financial freedom.

Breaking Free from Financial Stress

Financial stress can be a relentless burden, weighing down on every aspect of your life. It creeps into your thoughts during the day and even haunts your dreams at night. If you've ever lain awake, worrying about bills, debt, or an uncertain future, you're not alone. Many experience the same anxiety. In this section, we'll address this common enemy head-on and equip you with strategies to break free from financial stress.

Financial stress often stems from uncertainty, a lack of control, or overwhelming debt. It can affect your mental and emotional well-being, impacting not only your finances but also your relationships, health, and overall quality of life. It's a heavy load to carry, but it's not one you have to bear forever. Together, we'll explore the sources of your financial stress and tackle them with confidence.

Throughout my career, I've witnessed the incredible transformation that occurs when individuals regain control of their financial lives and release the burden of stress. This section is your opportunity to reclaim your peace of mind and take charge of your financial destiny.

Inside Money Rules, you'll learn practical techniques to manage your money and eliminate stress, by making effective financial decisions, and building resilience in the face of life's uncertainties.

Financial stress is not a life sentence. Remember that you're taking a crucial step towards a brighter, stress-free future. You'll have the knowledge to face financial challenges head-on and emerge stronger, more resilient, and ready to thrive.

Your Journey to Financial Freedom Begins

Congratulations! You've embarked on your journey to financial freedom. The decision to take control of your financial destiny is a powerful one, and it's a choice that can transform your life in remarkable ways. It's essential to understand that your journey is unique. Your goals, aspirations, and dreams are yours alone. You are the captain of this ship, and I'm here to be your trusted guide.

Many have walked this path before you, and they've experienced the profound changes that come with financial empowerment. Whether your dream is to retire comfortably, provide for your family, travel the world, or pursue your passions, financial freedom can make it possible. The journey may have its challenges, but it's also filled with opportunities, excitement, and the satisfaction of progress.

In the upcoming chapters, we'll explore the essential principles of Money Rules, a system designed to simplify the complexities of personal finance and guide you toward financial security and independence. Each chapter will unveil a new aspect of financial empowerment, equipping you with practical knowledge and actionable steps to move closer to your goals.

Your journey to financial freedom begins now. It's a journey that will not only reshape your financial future but also empower you to live life on your terms. So, let's set sail together, charting a course toward your financial aspirations. It's time to embrace the possibilities that lie ahead, make informed choices, and experience the freedom that comes with taking control of your financial destiny.

“The secret of getting ahead is getting started.”

- Mark Twain

CHAPTER 3

DEFINING YOUR FINANCIAL GOALS

The Importance of Setting Clear Goals

Setting clear financial goals is the cornerstone of achieving financial security and independence. Just as a ship needs a destination to chart its course, your financial journey requires direction. Without clear goals, your finances can drift aimlessly, leaving you vulnerable to financial uncertainty. In this section, we explore why setting goals is essential and how it can shape your financial future.

Clear goals provide a sense of purpose and motivation in your financial life. They give you something to strive for, whether it's buying a home, sending your children to college, or retiring comfortably. Having a vision of your financial future can inspire you to take action, make informed decisions, and stay committed to your long-term objectives.

Setting financial goals also brings clarity to your financial decision-making. It helps you prioritize your spending, savings, and investments based on what truly matters to you. With defined goals, you can distinguish between needs and wants, making it easier to allocate your resources effectively.

Moreover, clear financial goals act as a measuring stick for your progress. They enable you to track your achievements and celebrate milestones along the way. This sense of accomplishment can boost your confidence and reinforce your commitment to your financial journey.

Short-term, Medium-Term, and Long-Term Goals

Goals come in different shapes and sizes, and they often fall into three broad categories: short-term, medium-term, and long-term. Short-term goals typically span the next 12 months and may include paying off credit card debt, saving for a vacation, or building an emergency fund. Medium-term goals, ranging from two to five years, might involve buying a car, starting a business, or saving for a down payment on a home. Long-term goals extend beyond five years and encompass major milestones like retirement planning and legacy building.

Each category of goals plays a unique role in your financial journey. Short-term goals provide immediate gratification and financial stability, while medium-term goals offer a sense of progress and achievement. Long-term goals, on the other hand, provide the vision of a secure and fulfilling future.

Balancing these goals is crucial, as they interact and influence one another. Achieving short-term goals can free up resources for medium-term objectives, while medium-term success contributes to the realization of long-term dreams. By strategically aligning your goals across these time frames, you create a holistic financial plan that propels you toward security and independence.

Exploring practical strategies for setting and achieving short-term, medium-term, and long-term goals should only be undertaken once the basic fundamentals of your money management plan are solidly in place. None of this needs to be rushed. However, it is very important to get the basics in place and establish a solid foundation to build upon.

Whether you're focused on immediate financial stability or long-term retirement planning, you need to equip yourself with the tools to define your goals and set yourself on the path to financial security.

Your Path to Financial Security

Your financial security is the sum of your financial choices, and it begins with the clarity of your goals. While financial security may sound like an elusive concept, it's within your grasp. It's about creating a life where you have the resources and confidence to weather life's storms and pursue your dreams. Your path to financial security begins with defining your goals and building a roadmap to achieve them.

Financial security is not about adhering to rigid budgets or sacrificing your present enjoyment for an uncertain future. It's about making informed decisions that align with your values and aspirations. It's about understanding that financial freedom is not a destination but a continuous journey.

The reason why Money Rules works is because there are some practical strategies, tools, and mindset shifts that will help you pave the way to financial security. From managing debt and investing wisely to creating multiple streams of income, you'll discover the steps to building a solid financial foundation. The journey may have its challenges, but it's a journey that ultimately leads to empowerment, peace of mind, and the realization of your financial goals.

The purpose of Money Rules was to create a money management system that would provide a realistic approach to managing money and eliminating debt. The initial goal was centred on eliminating debt in the fastest possible manner without the need to refinance, remortgage, beg, borrow or steal, get a second or third job, eat baked beans or ramen noodles for the next ten years, sell a kidney, or have to move back in with the parents. The purpose of the program was to establish a comfortable baseline from which to operate and implement future planning. It actually exceeded that!

Remember, financial security is not an abstract concept; it's a tangible reality that you can create for yourself. By embracing the power of clear goals and understanding their role in your financial journey, you're taking a significant step toward a future filled with confidence, independence, and the freedom to live life on your terms.

“Your time is limited,

so don’t waste it living someone else’s life.”

- Steve Jobs

CHAPTER 4

THE ROLE OF MONEY RULES

Introducing Money Rules: Your Financial Ally

In the vast sea of financial advice and tools, Money Rules emerges as a guiding light, your unwavering ally in the pursuit of financial freedom. This chapter introduces you to a transformative system designed to empower you, regardless of your financial background or expertise. Money Rules is not just another financial program; it's your trusted companion on the journey to financial security and independence.

Money Rules is built on the foundation of simplicity, accessibility, and results. It distils the complexities of financial management into an easy-to-follow system that empowers you to take control of your financial destiny. Whether you're navigating the challenges of debt, planning for retirement, or striving to create wealth, Money Rules offers a personalized approach tailored to your unique financial goals.

What sets Money Rules apart is its commitment to your financial well-being. It doesn't rely on a one-size-fits-all solution but rather embraces the idea that financial security is deeply personal. Money Rules adapts to your needs, aspirations, and circumstances, providing you with the guidance and tools required to achieve your financial dreams.

As we explore the facets of Money Rules in the pages that follow, you'll discover how this system can serve as a compass, steering you toward financial freedom. It's not just about numbers and spreadsheets, or algorithms and optimisation; it's about gaining the confidence and knowledge to make informed financial decisions. Money Rules is your financial ally, ready to accompany you on this exciting journey toward financial security. It puts you back in control of your money, your decisions, and your financial certainty.

The Unique Features of Money Rules

Money Rules boasts a set of unique features that make it stand out in the world of personal finance. These features are designed to simplify complex financial concepts, provide actionable insights, and empower you to take control of your money. By understanding what sets Money Rules apart, you'll gain clarity on how this system can benefit your financial journey.

One of the standout features of Money Rules is its personalized approach. Instead of offering generic financial advice, Money Rules tailors its recommendations to your specific financial goals, priorities, and circumstances. It's like having a personal money advisor in your pocket, ready to provide guidance whenever you need it.

Money Rules also places a strong emphasis on simplicity and accessibility. You don't need to be a financial expert to use this system effectively. Its user-friendly interface and straightforward guidance ensure that anyone, regardless of their financial literacy level, can harness its power.

Moreover, the Money Rules program is not a one-time solution but an ongoing companion. It adapts to your changing financial situation, offering continuous support and updates as you progress on your financial journey. It's a dynamic system that evolves with you, ensuring that you stay on track toward your goals.

Money Rules is:

- Not a '6 week course', coaching, budgeting tool, or a short-term training program.
- It is a personalized system tailored to your unique financial situation.
- It is designed to optimize outcomes by leveraging your provided information, minimizing interest expenses, and saving valuable time.
- Money Rules is incredibly user-friendly, with a simple data entry process that requires only periodic updates.

Why Money Rules Matters to You

You might be wondering why Money Rules is relevant to your life. The answer is simple: it matters because it can change the trajectory of your financial future. Money Rules matters to you because it's the key to unlocking financial security, independence, and the freedom to live life on your terms. Time is the greatest asset that cannot be bought, and the program shows that the longer you wait, the more your future will cost.

For too long, the financial industry has relied on complex jargon and intimidating strategies that often leave individuals feeling overwhelmed and powerless. Money Rules breaks through these barriers, placing the control back in your hands. It matters to you because it empowers you to make confident, informed decisions about your money.

Money Rules matters because it aligns with your desire for financial stability and independence. It's a system that acknowledges your unique challenges and aspirations, offering solutions that resonate with your goals and values. By using Money Rules, you're not just managing money; you're forging a path to your financial dreams.

Money Rules will benefit your financial journey. From setting clear goals to making informed investment decisions, you'll discover the practical tools and strategies that Money Rules offers. By the end of this book, you'll understand why Money Rules is more than a financial program—it's your partner in achieving the financial security and independence you deserve.

“Money is a terrible master
but an excellent servant.”
- P.T. Barnum

CHAPTER 5

CREATING YOUR FINANCIAL BLUEPRINT

The Foundation of Financial Success

At the core of any successful financial journey lies a robust foundation—a blueprint that guides your path to financial security. Traditional budgeting approaches elicit feelings of fear or restriction. Money Rules offers you something entirely different: the power to craft your financial future. It's not about budgets and deprivations, but about building a blueprint that empowers you to achieve your dreams and aspirations.

Think of this chapter as the starting point of your financial adventure. We're not here to tell you to tighten your belt or cut out your favourite indulgences. Instead, we'll guide you through the process of creating a financial blueprint that aligns with your unique goals and values. Money Rules is your partner in this endeavour, providing you with the tools and knowledge to pave the way for financial success.

Financial success isn't about deprivation; it's about conscious choices that lead to financial freedom. It is about modifying behaviours. Small changes can have big outcomes. Just like 'small hinges swing big doors'. We'll help you reframe your perspective on managing money, showing you that it's not about giving up what you love but rather channelling your resources toward what truly matters to you. Money Rules can help you build a solid financial foundation, step by step.

So, are you ready to start crafting your financial future with confidence? Let's embark on this journey together, where budgets are a thing of the past, and financial blueprints are your passport to freedom.

Creating Your Future With Money Rules

Imagine having a clear roadmap to your financial dreams—one that takes into account your unique aspirations and challenges. With Money Rules, this vision becomes your reality. In this section, we'll explore how Money Rules can help you create a brighter and more secure financial future.

Traditional budgeting often falls short of addressing long-term financial goals. Money Rules, on the other hand, is designed to guide you not just in managing your day-to-day finances but also in achieving your future dreams. It empowers you to set clear financial goals, plan for major life events, and build wealth over time.

One of the key differences between Money Rules and traditional budgeting is that it fosters a positive and proactive approach to financial planning. Instead of focusing on restrictions or limitations, Money Rules encourages you to align your financial decisions with your values and priorities. You are encouraged to be inspired and dream bigger, better, faster.

Money Rules serves as your financial compass, pointing the way to a future filled with security, independence, and the freedom to pursue your passions.

Overcoming Common Budgeting Challenges

Budgeting has its fair share of challenges. There are two types of people who start budgeting. Those who want to take control of their money flows, and those who know they are already in trouble and are looking to a budget as a means of identifying how it can help them. Budgets can be simple if used for a simple cash flow.

Many people view it as a daunting task, fraught with limitations and discipline. In this section, we'll address the common challenges associated with budgeting and how Money Rules offers a refreshing alternative.

One of the most significant challenges people face with budgeting is the fear of restriction. It often feels like a set of rules designed to limit your spending. Money Rules, in contrast, is all about empowerment and choice. It allows you to make informed decisions about your money while staying true to your goals, dreams and desires.

Another hurdle in traditional budgeting is the feeling of guilt or failure when you deviate from the budget. Budgets can also be restrictive, confronting reality checks, fearsome, and loathsome. Often creating a budget is already an admission of defeat, failure, and even embarrassment. Budgets have an essence of hopelessness and despair like standing on the deck of a sinking ship waiting to be saved and knowing that no one is coming.

Budgets are a starting point and an acceptance that there is a problem that needs to be taken seriously. For many, it is also the beginning of an agonising journey.

Money Rules, on the other hand, is designed to be flexible, recognizing that life is full of unexpected twists and turns. It adapts to your changing circumstances and provides guidance that aligns with your financial goals. Just like a GPS system that guides your travels, Money Rules will steer you back on track. The ultimate goal of personal money management is to be financially secure and the goal of Money Rules is to lead you along that path and show you the future.

Money Rules offers a solution to these common budgeting challenges. It's time to leave behind the negativity associated with budgeting and embrace a financial approach that empowers you to create the life you've always dreamed of.

“The only true wisdom is in knowing you know nothing.”

- Socrates

CHAPTER 6

DEBT DEMYSTIFIED

Understanding Debt and Its Impact

Debt can often feel like a shadow lurking in the background, casting a cloud over your financial well-being. In this chapter, we'll shed light on debt, helping you understand its various forms and the profound impact it can have on your financial journey. Whether it's student loans, credit card debt, or a mortgage, we'll demystify the world of debt and show you how to navigate it with confidence.

Debt isn't inherently good or bad; it's a tool that can be used wisely or mismanaged. We'll explore the difference between "good" and "bad" debt and how to distinguish between the two. Understanding the role debt plays in your life is crucial to making informed financial decisions.

One of the key principles of Money Rules is to empower you to take control of your financial destiny. This includes tackling debt head-on and using it strategically to achieve your goals. By the end of this section, you'll have a clearer picture of your debt landscape and its implications for your financial future.

The first step to overcoming any challenge is understanding it. Debt is no exception. By gaining insight into the nature of debt and its consequences, you'll be better equipped to make choices that align with your financial aspirations.

Strategies to Tackle Debt Head-On

Debt may seem insurmountable at times, but it's important to remember that you have the power to conquer it. We'll dive into practical strategies to tackle debt head-on. Whether you're dealing with high-interest credit card debt or a substantial student loan, Money Rules provides you with a roadmap to become debt-free.

We'll explore the concept of debt consolidation, a method that can simplify your debt repayment journey and potentially save you money. Additionally, you'll discover techniques to negotiate with creditors and reduce the burden of interest charges.

Debt consolidation is a powerful strategy. It's a financial approach that can significantly streamline your debt repayment process while offering the potential to save you a substantial amount of money in the long run. Debt consolidation involves combining multiple debts, such as credit card balances or personal loans, into a single, more manageable loan with a lower interest rate. By doing so, you can simplify your financial life by consolidating various monthly payments into one, making it easier to keep track of your debt and stay on top of your payments.

One of the key benefits of debt consolidation is the potential for substantial interest savings. High-interest debts, such as credit card balances, can quickly accumulate, causing you to pay a significant amount in interest charges over time. With debt consolidation, you may qualify for a lower interest rate on the consolidated loan, which means more of your monthly payment goes towards reducing the principal balance rather than paying interest. This can lead to faster debt reduction and less money spent on interest over the life of the loan.

Negotiating with creditors can be a valuable skill in your financial toolkit, as it allows you to work towards reducing the burden of interest charges, late fees, and potentially even the principal amount owed. Whether you're dealing with credit card companies, personal loan providers, or other creditors, learning how to negotiate can help you secure more favourable terms and, in some cases, create a more manageable repayment plan. We'll provide practical tips and strategies to help you navigate these conversations confidently and assertively, ultimately working towards a more financially secure future.

Before we delve into the realm of negotiation, it's essential to recognize that Money Rules was meticulously designed to minimize the need for debt consolidation or renegotiation, making them options of last resort. If you find yourself in a financial situation where these alternatives appear to be the only viable paths forward, it's crucial to consider seeking professional financial guidance.

However, it's important to note that if you've reached a point where debt consolidation or renegotiation becomes your primary financial strategy, Money Rules may not align with your current needs and circumstances. This program is ideally suited for individuals looking to proactively manage their finances, optimize their financial stability, and reduce their reliance on debt-related solutions. If you've already ventured deep into the realm of debt management, we encourage you to explore other financial resources better tailored to your specific situation.

Navigating financial conversations with creditors confidently and assertively is a crucial skill that can have a profound impact on your journey to financial security. To help you achieve this, we'll offer a range of practical tips and strategies that empower you to take control of these discussions effectively.

First and foremost, we'll emphasize the importance of preparation. Before engaging in any conversation with creditors, it's essential to gather all relevant information about your debt, including account details, outstanding balances, and payment history. Armed with this knowledge, you'll approach the negotiation table with confidence, as you'll have a clear understanding of your financial position and the specifics of your debt.

One key strategy we'll explore is the art of effective communication. It's important to articulate your financial goals and challenges clearly and persuasively. By expressing your commitment to resolving your debts and your desire to work collaboratively with creditors, you'll foster a more positive and cooperative atmosphere during negotiations.

Additionally, remain persistent and patient. Negotiations with creditors may not always yield immediate results, but by maintaining a persistent yet respectful approach, you'll demonstrate your commitment to finding a mutually beneficial solution. Patience is also crucial, as it allows you to carefully consider offers and proposals, ensuring they align with your long-term financial goals.

Furthermore, we'll suggest negotiation tactics and techniques, such as proposing debt repayment plans, requesting interest rate reductions, or negotiating settlements. These strategies can help you secure more favourable terms and alleviate the financial burden of high-interest debts.

Ultimately, the goal is to empower you with the skills and confidence needed to navigate these financial conversations effectively. By doing so, you'll be well on your way to achieving a more financially secure future, free from the overwhelming weight of debt and interest charges.

All this while keeping in mind that the aim of Money Rules is to prioritize a debt schedule and to optimize for elimination in order to achieve the lowest interest payable in the shortest period of time. Consolidation is not considered necessary although it may yield some short term gains.

Money Rules encourages a proactive approach to debt management. Instead of letting debt control your life, you'll learn how to take control of your debt. The goal isn't just to become debt-free but also to use your newfound financial freedom to pursue your dreams and aspirations.

You'll find that Money Rules isn't just about managing debt; its priority is about eliminating it so that you stop paying wasted money in interest to the lenders. Using Money Rules means you'll be equipped with practical tools and strategies to embark far more quickly on your debt-free journey with confidence.

Another option available in the market is the approach where a company takes over your income to pay off your debts on your behalf. While this strategy is promoted as effective on television, many customers I've spoken with have expressed dissatisfaction due to high fees and minimal living allowances. This often leaves them struggling to make ends meet. In my view, it's an unnecessary and expensive solution. For individuals genuinely committed to securing their financial future, debt consolidation or debt management should be considered as a last resort.

It's worth noting that most services only administer their assistance while clients are paying ongoing fees.

In contrast, Money Rules offers lifetime access, providing a comprehensive financial solution that empowers individuals to take control of their finances and secure their financial future without the burden of perpetual fees.

Debt-Free Living with Money Rules

Imagine a life free from the weight of debt—a life where your financial decisions are driven by your aspirations, not your obligations. Money Rules is your guide to debt-free living, and in this section, we'll explore how this transformative approach can change your financial landscape.

Debt-free living isn't just about being debt-free; it's about reaping the benefits of your financial discipline. We'll look into the concept of financial freedom and how it can enhance your quality of life.

Money Rules empowers you to make choices that align with your values and aspirations, giving you the freedom to pursue your passions, travel, invest, and secure your future. By implementing the principles of Money Rules, you'll not only eliminate debt but also unlock a world of possibilities.

Imagine the plans you can start making towards holidays or purchases. What would you do? Where would you go? We've shown users how to incorporate these plans directly into the program so that there's no future bill shock. Everything is planned for the long term. Whenever I had client meetings about retirement planning, my first question was always about what they wanted to do in retirement. It's funny how two people who have lived together for decades could have opposing ideas about their dreams and not be aware of each other's goals.

Debt-free living is not a distant dream; it's within your reach with the right knowledge and approach. Discover how Money Rules can help you break free from the chains of debt and step into a life filled with financial security, confidence, and boundless opportunities. Start creating your future plans now.

If you're eager to get started – and we hope you are – head over to https://moneyrules.com.au/ria

There, you'll find a video that will guide you through the initial steps. Follow the recommendations, enter your details, and set yourself on the path to financial empowerment.

"Knowing is not enough, we must apply.
Willing is not enough, we must do."
- Bruce Lee

CHAPTER 7

WEALTH BUILDING MADE SIMPLE

The Power of Saving and Investing

Saving and investing are the twin engines that drive wealth creation. In this chapter, we'll delve into the profound impact that these financial strategies can have on your future. Whether you're starting with a small nest egg or have substantial resources at your disposal, Money Rules will guide you through the steps to harness the power of saving and investing.

We'll begin by exploring the concept of saving and how it lays the foundation for your financial security. Money Rules agrees with the importance of building an emergency fund and setting aside money for short-term goals. These practices not only provide peace of mind but also create a stable financial platform from which to launch your wealth-building journey.

Money Rules teaches you how to strike a balance between these two essential components of wealth building, ensuring that you're prepared for both short-term financial needs and long-term financial aspirations.

How Money Rules Helps You Grow Wealth

Money Rules isn't just about managing your finances; it's about growing your wealth systematically. In this part of the chapter, we'll explore how Money Rules provides you with the tools and strategies to multiply your assets over time. Whether you're looking to retire comfortably, fund your children's education, or leave a legacy, Money Rules is your ally on the path to wealth.

Although the main purpose of the Money Rules program is to manage money and eliminate debt, it also introduces you to the concept of a "wealth amplifier," a powerful tool within Money Rules that accelerates your wealth-building journey.

Too often, people will pay off debt and then use that money to fund a lifestyle of excess. By focusing on predictable results, you'll discover a new way to approach wealth creation—one that reduces stress and enhances your financial security.

Lifestyle planning is a strategy aimed at ensuring that you'll have enough financial resources in the future to maintain your desired lifestyle during retirement.

It involves two key steps: first, envisioning the kind of lifestyle you want, and then making sure you have the necessary funds to support it. The ultimate goal is to avoid the unsettling scenario of running out of money before you reach the end of your life.

Money Rules leverages a proven mathematical formula to guide your financial decisions, ensuring that each step you take aligns with your goals. Inside the program, we'll delve into how this formula works and why it's a game-changer for your financial future.

You'll be equipped with the knowledge and tools to make your money work for you, rather than the other way around. Money Rules transforms your financial outlook, moving you from uncertainty to confidence, from stress to peace of mind, and from a life of financial constraints to one of boundless possibilities.

Building a Solid Financial Future

Building wealth isn't just about accumulating assets; it's about securing your financial future and achieving the life you desire. Money Rules is your blueprint for creating a solid financial foundation that will support your dreams and aspirations.

You will quickly understand the importance of having a clear financial plan and how Money Rules simplifies the planning process. You'll learn how to set specific financial goals, both short-term and long-term, and develop a roadmap to achieve them.

Money Rules also emphasize the value of consistent, disciplined action. The core function of the program is to eliminate debt in order to free up money for wealth creation. Once debt is out of the way, and using the available funds, we'll explore how regular contributions to your financial future can yield significant results over time. Whether you're saving for retirement, a dream vacation, or your children's education, Money Rules provides a path to get there.

Discover how Money Rules doesn't just stop at eliminating debt; it ignites the next chapter in your journey to financial prosperity. As you've already seen, there are inspiring success stories of individuals who've harnessed this system. You'll experience more than just the remarkable savings they've accomplished. Their transformation extends beyond debt elimination, offering a glimpse into the uncharted territory of financial freedom that is a possibility for many.

With the burden of debt lifted, anyone can transition from a mindset of scarcity to one of abundance. Yet, this newfound liberation is only the beginning, not the end. Money Rules sets the stage for your financial evolution, making your dreams of a secure financial future not just possible but attainable. Embrace the guidance of Money Rules and embark on this exciting journey towards lasting prosperity. Your financial destiny awaits – it's time to seize it.

“Money isn’t the most important thing in life, but it’s reasonably close to oxygen on the ‘gotta have it’ scale.”

- Zig Ziglar

CHAPTER 8

NAVIGATING LIFE'S FINANCIAL CHALLENGES

Preparing for Life's Unexpected Turns

Life is unpredictable, and sometimes, it throws us curveballs we never saw coming. Money Rules equips you with the tools and strategies to prepare for life's unexpected financial challenges. Whether it's a sudden medical expense, a major home repair, a life-changing experience, or a job loss, Money Rules ensures that you have a safety net in place.

We'll begin by discussing the importance of building an emergency fund—an essential component of financial security. Money Rules recommends you establish and grow this fund, providing you with peace of mind knowing that you're financially prepared for unexpected expenses. Given the recent global concerns, it makes sense to set aside funds to meet expenses for six to twelve months. Having said that, funds that are not actively decreasing your debt should be considered as a loss. An emergency fund that provides immediate access as well as investment growth is a worthwhile achievement.

Beyond emergency funds, we recommend that you consider the various insurance instruments that are available to help you navigate life's financial uncertainties. It should go without saying that general insurance policies to cover household and motor vehicles should be in place.

Making wise insurance choices, and creating a robust financial plan that anticipates and mitigates potential setbacks, provides for clarity in planning. You should contact the relevant providers for these insurances and undertake a needs analysis. Insurance is only of value if it is in place on the day it is needed.

Money Rules recommends you take control of your financial future, even in the face of life's unexpected challenges. It's about being proactive, ensuring your financial well-being, and maintaining the freedom to thrive, no matter what life throws your way.

Safeguarding Your Future with Money Rules

Safeguarding your future is a crucial aspect of financial independence. We'll explore the role of insurance, estate planning, and risk management in securing your family's future.

As a former financial adviser, I highly recommend you make informed decisions about life insurance, disability coverage, long-term care insurance and income protection. The insurance isn't so much for you, but to protect your assets and provide for your loved ones and ensure their financial security in case of unforeseen events.

Estate planning is another vital component of securing your family's future.

In this section, we'll embark on a crucial aspect of financial planning that often gets overlooked but is of paramount importance: estate planning. It's important to consider the significance of wills, trusts, and beneficiary designations that play a pivotal role in assisting you in crafting a comprehensive estate plan that not only reflects your wishes but also safeguards your legacy.

Wills are the cornerstone of any estate plan, outlining your preferences regarding the distribution of your assets, guardianship of minors, and even the care of your beloved pets. We'll discuss the importance of creating a well-structured will that leaves no room for ambiguity and ensures that your assets are distributed according to your desires.

Trusts, on the other hand, offer a more versatile approach to estate planning. There are various types of trusts available and each has its distinct advantages, such as probate, protecting assets, and providing for special needs beneficiaries. You should engage suitably qualified advisers to establish and manage trusts seamlessly, allowing you to tailor your estate plan to your unique circumstances.

Beneficiary designations, often associated with retirement accounts and insurance policies, are another critical component of estate planning. Be sure to designate beneficiaries effectively, ensuring that your assets smoothly transition to your chosen heirs while minimizing tax implications.

Create an estate plan that not only addresses your immediate financial concerns but also safeguards your wealth for future generations. It's a comprehensive approach to financial planning that considers not just your financial well-being today but also your enduring legacy.

It's about creating a legacy of financial security that transcends generations.

Thriving Through Life's Ups and Downs

Life isn't just about weathering the storms—it's also about seizing the opportunities and thriving during the ups. In this final part of the chapter, we'll explore how Money Rules empowers you to embrace life's joys and make the most of your financial independence.

Life is an intricate tapestry of experiences, a blend of challenges and triumphs, setbacks and victories. While the financial world often focuses on preparing for the storms, it's equally essential to seize the opportunities and relish the moments of joy and prosperity. In this concluding section of the chapter, we'll embark on a journey of exploration, one that emphasizes not just surviving but thriving during life's ups.

Money Rules is more than just a financial tool; it's a companion for life's incredible moments. With the solid financial foundation, it helps you build, you'll be better equipped to savour the joys of life, whether it's travelling to exotic destinations, indulging in your favourite hobbies, or creating unforgettable memories with your loved ones. Financial independence isn't just about security; it's about the freedom to embrace life's pleasures without reservation.

Set financial goals that encompass not only your responsibilities and obligations but also your dreams and aspirations. Money Rules empowers you to outline a path that leads not just to stability but to a life filled with the experiences and adventures you desire. It provides the framework not just for bills but also for experiences, allowing you to create cherished moments that define a life well-lived.

Furthermore, consider the art of mindful spending and the significance of aligning your financial choices with your values and aspirations. Money Rules encourages you to make conscious decisions that reflect your priorities, ensuring that your resources are allocated to what truly matters to you. It's about making choices that enhance your overall well-being and contribute to a life rich in purpose and fulfilment.

As we wrap up this chapter, remember that your journey to financial independence isn't solely about the destination—it's about embracing each moment along the way. Money Rules is your guide to not only weathering life's storms but also basking in its sunny days. It's a tool that empowers you to make the most of your financial independence, allowing you to lead a life filled with opportunities, joy, and contentment.

Are you planning for major life events, such as buying a home, funding your children's education, or taking that dream vacation? Money Rules isn't just about saving for the future; it's about living life to the fullest today.

You'll see that Money Rules is not just a financial system—it's a lifestyle that empowers you to navigate life's challenges, safeguard your future, and thrive through every season. It's your passport to a life of abundance, joy, and financial freedom.

"The best way to predict your future is to create it."

- Abraham Lincoln

CHAPTER 9

YOUR FINANCIAL TRANSFORMATION

Your Journey to Financial Independence

Congratulations! You've embarked on a transformative journey toward financial independence, and you've chosen the path guided by Money Rules. In this chapter, we'll explore the incredible transformation that awaits you. Financial freedom is not a distant dream—it's your reality in the making.

We'll begin by reflecting on your unique journey—the challenges you've overcome, the goals you've set, and the progress you've achieved. Money Rules has been your trusted companion throughout, providing guidance, support, and a clear roadmap.

Think about the power of discipline and consistency, which are the cornerstones of your financial transformation. Money Rules empowers you to make intentional choices, take control of your finances, and build a future filled with possibilities.

Your journey to financial independence is not just about reaching a destination—it's about the growth, learning, and empowerment you've experienced along the way. With Money Rules, your journey is a testament to your determination and resilience.

Celebrating Milestones Along the Way

In life, it's essential to celebrate your wins, no matter how small or significant. Your financial transformation with Money Rules is no exception. In this part of the chapter, we'll explore the milestones you've achieved and how to savour each victory.

Consider the power of gratitude and reflection. By acknowledging your progress, you'll find motivation and inspiration to keep moving forward. Money Rules ensures that every step you take is a step toward your financial goals.

There's a joy in achieving your short-term, medium-term, and long-term goals. Whether it's paying off debt, building an emergency fund, or investing for your retirement, each accomplishment brings you closer to your vision of financial independence. At each milestone, take credit and treat yourself.

The Confidence and Peace of Mind You Deserve

As you near the end of this transformative journey, we'll explore how your newfound financial independence has reduced stress and anxiety related to money. You're no longer held captive by financial uncertainty; instead, you have a clear vision and a roadmap to follow.

One of the most important aspects you will feel is the sense of empowerment that comes with financial control. Money Rules has equipped you with the knowledge and tools to make informed decisions, negotiate confidently, and create the future you desire.

By now, you'll realize that you deserve the confidence and peace of mind that Money Rules provides. You're no longer a bystander in your financial journey—you're the driver, charting your course toward a life of abundance and fulfilment.

"If you wait until tomorrow,
today is a lost opportunity."
- Nobby Kleinman

CHAPTER 10

TAKING ACTION WITH MONEY RULES

Getting Started with Money Rules Today

Now that you've gained a deep understanding of Money Rules and the transformation it can bring to your financial life, it's time to take action. The journey to financial independence begins with a single step, and that step is to register here https://moneyrules.com.au/ria

In this section, we'll guide you through the process of getting started with Money Rules. You'll learn how to set up your account, input your financial information, and what you can expect in your report.

Your Exclusive Offer: Results In Advance

As a token of my appreciation for embarking on this journey, I am thrilled to present you with a valuable offer: Results In Advance. Yes, the very same offer I had already made earlier. This special program is designed to accelerate your progress toward financial freedom.

Results In Advance is your link to work directly with financial experts who understand the power of Money Rules. You'll receive a personalized report giving you insights into where you are now and where you could be.

Results In Advance is always the first step toward a deeper conversation if you qualify. As much as we would like to work with everyone, not everyone will qualify for various reasons. That's rare, but it can and does happen. It may be that someone is not actually in a great financial position to take advantage of what Money Rules can do for them.

It may be that they failed to fully complete the online form and have just wasted our time as well as their own. And in some instances, they just don't turn up for an appointment.

I'm certain that because you have read this far, you are not that sort of person. In fact, congratulations for reading all the way through here. It tells me something about you. You are committed, you are interested, and perhaps even intrigued to know more about how your situation can be improved. Possibly even excited by the prospect of having your own unique financial plan created specifically for you.

Results In Advance is the precursor to Money Rules. It is the data collection centre that allows us to shorten the time to provide you with your report. Without this data, the program is incomplete and we are unable to do anything without the information.

You will see a copy of the report in the video on the application page. It is a single, one page report. It's a powerful visualisation that will fast-track your path to financial independence. And it looks like this one...

Prepared for
Client Demo

Date Prepared: 07/06/2021

MONEY RULES
Your Choices. Your Future

You are here

Results In Advance

You could be here

	Current	Money Rules
Total Debts	353,333	353,333
Total Interest	265,122.74	169,357.39
Years	30	21.08

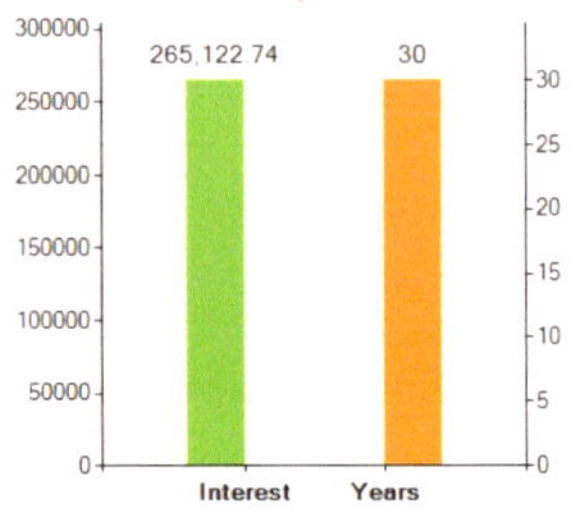

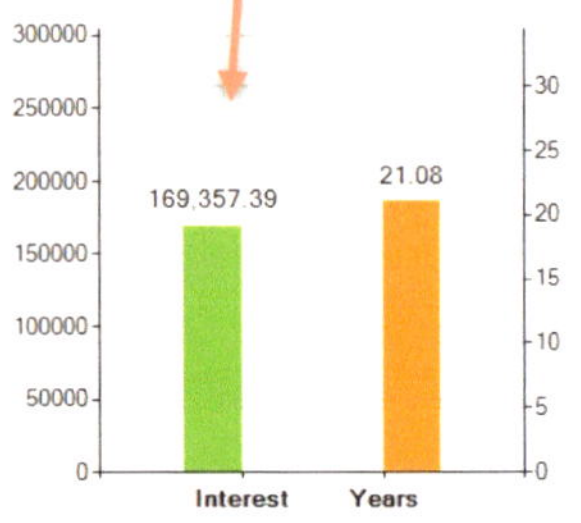

	Current	Money Rules
Interest Saved	0	95,765.35
Years Saved	0	8.92
Debt Free	Mar. 2051	Mar. 2042

Future Value

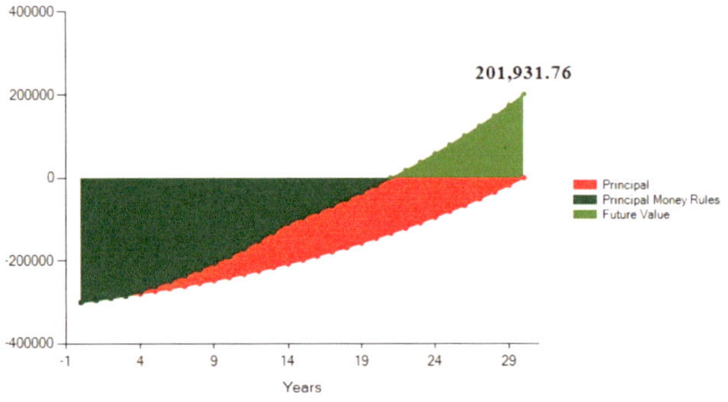

No two results will ever be the same due to numerous factors

Your Financial Freedom Awaits

The journey you've undertaken with Money Rules is not just about managing money—it's about reclaiming your financial freedom.

Within the program, we'll explore the possibilities that financial independence opens up for you and your loved ones. Imagine a life where you can pursue your passions, travel the world and provide for your family without constraints.

We'll discuss the peace of mind that comes with knowing you're prepared for life's unexpected challenges. Financial security is your shield against uncertainty, and Money Rules is your trusted ally.

By the end of this section, you'll be fueled with excitement and anticipation. Your financial freedom is not a distant dream—it's a tangible reality that you can achieve with the support of Money Rules and Results In Advance.

Your future awaits, and it's brighter than ever.

"If it is to be, it is up to me."

- William Johnsen

CONCLUSION

The Future Is Yours to Create

As we conclude this transformative journey through the world of Money Rules, I want to leave you with a powerful message: the future is yours to create. You hold the pen to write the next chapters of your financial story.

Throughout this book, we've explored the unique challenges that many face on their financial journeys and discovered how Money Rules can be your guiding light towards financial independence. It's not about relying on anyone else—it's about taking control of your destiny.

The future you envision is within your reach, and it starts with the choices you make today. Money Rules empowers you to make informed decisions, set clear goals, and build a solid financial foundation.

So, as you turn the page and step into the future, remember that you have the knowledge, tools, and determination to shape the life you desire. Your financial freedom is not a distant dream—it's a reality you can create, one smart financial choice at a time.

Embracing a Life of Financial Freedom

Embracing a life of financial freedom means stepping into a world where you have the power to live life on your terms. It's about shedding the shackles of financial stress and embracing the limitless possibilities that await you.

You will find out what it truly means to live a life of financial freedom. It's not just about money; it's about having the confidence, peace of mind, and freedom to pursue your passions and dreams.

You will become one of the real-life stories of individuals who have embraced financial freedom with the help of Money Rules. These inspiring journeys will show you that it's possible, regardless of your starting point.

When you have a clear road map and blueprint to work to, you'll be ready to step into a new chapter of your life—one filled with financial abundance, security, and the freedom to live life on your terms.

Your First Step Toward Financial Independence

Taking your first step toward financial independence is a monumental leap, signifying your unwavering commitment to seizing control of your financial destiny and crafting a brighter future. To embark on this transformational journey, there's a crucial and immediate action you should take.

It all starts with a powerful shift in your mindset—from apprehension about the future to an enthusiastic embrace of the possibilities ahead. This shift empowers you to create a life designed by your aspirations, rather than living one scripted by others. It's about reclaiming authority over the narrative of your life, ensuring that you are the master of your destiny.

Results In Advance - How Do You Get Started?

Once you've committed to this life-changing journey, the next crucial step is to set clear financial goals and embrace the invaluable tools of Money Rules and Results In Advance. It's time to put your newfound knowledge into action.

Your initial move is to visit https://MoneyRules.com.au/ria which will take you to a registration page and an informative video guiding you through the next steps.

Essentially, this involves gathering your financial details and noting them down on the downloadable Categories pages. You don't need to fill in every line, just those relevant to your situation.

The process may seem unconventional, but it serves a specific purpose, which I'll explain when we meet. Once you've completed this task, it's a simple matter of transferring that data to the online form.

When you've filled in the necessary details, simply hit the SUBMIT button at the end of the page, and your information will be securely transmitted to Money Rules to create your Results In Advance report. You can expect to receive this report within about 48 business hours, whenever possible.

As you've already seen, the Results In Advance report, a concise one-page summary, is your initial milestone in this journey. It offers insights into your current financial status and highlights opportunities for improvement. Most people are amazed by the potential modifications that can significantly enhance their financial standing.

Think of the Results In Advance report as your financial diagnosis, marking the transition point where insights evolve into a tangible action plan.

If the Results in Advance report ignites your curiosity and motivates you to learn more, we'll proceed to schedule a comprehensive paid meeting, known as Fast Track, lasting approximately an hour. Before this meeting, you'll receive a brief questionnaire to complete and return 24 hours in advance, providing valuable insights.

Fast Track

Our Fast Track meeting, aptly named for its purpose, is designed to fast-track your journey to financial clarity and empowerment. It's human nature to be inquisitive, to crave knowledge about what the future holds. We're all drawn to that irresistible urge, driven by an instinctive curiosity. After all, wouldn't you want to know? That's why our Fast Track meeting offers you a crystal ball into your financial future, a peek that no one can resist needing or wanting to see.

During this session, we meticulously dissect your financial situation, providing a comprehensive diagnosis of your financial health. You'll gain a profound understanding of how your personalized plan report came to be, and together, we'll craft recommendations to elevate your financial well-being. This journey is marked by your active involvement; you're in the driver's seat while Money Rules guides you like a North Star.

Every step of this transformational journey is under your control, each stage a building block toward financial clarity. While our meeting is typically one-on-one, we encourage the participation of all involved in the decision process, recognizing the strength that comes from shared goals.

Rest assured, the entire meeting will be recorded for your convenience, ensuring you can review it at your leisure. We'll also provide a transcript of the video and a personalized report containing the recommendations, including each of the eight crucial reports. This transformational journey is a collaboration, with you as the captain navigating toward your financial plan.

As we conclude this meeting, you'll depart armed with knowledge and support to turn your financial aspirations into reality. Your journey commences at this point, and the future ahead shines brighter than ever before.

By the meeting's end, most of your pressing questions will find answers, leaving you with a renewed sense of hope and a blueprint for your financial future. You'll have a much clearer vision of what's achievable, all within your current income's reach.

Remember, the Results In Advance report serves as your starting point, and the sooner you begin, the quicker you'll gain insight into your financial future. It's like having a crystal ball view of your lifestyle and the possibilities it holds.

"Money is only a tool. It will take you wherever you wish, but it will not replace you as the driver."

- Ayn Rand

LEAD BY EXAMPLE

Whenever I do a presentation, I use the first person I ever introduced into the program. And that was back in 2008. I found her on Facebook one morning at about 2 a.m. Now, that's not an abnormal time for me, but I asked her what she was doing up at that time. She told me they had just upgraded their family car to a people mover as a safety factor because of the children. But she was concerned and worried about it being repossessed and couldn't sleep.

I asked her why would it be repossessed and she explained that she had done the family budget before the purchase, and everything looked fine. They even qualified without a problem for the car loan based on her figures. But after they arrived home, her mind had gone into overdrive and she was concerned something wasn't sitting right in the numbers. And because of that, she was not sleeping and really stressing about the car being taken away.

There's not much you can do at 2 a.m. so I told her to take a deep breath, relax, and get some sleep and I would come over on the following Friday to go through it with her. She was to have all her paperwork ready to go so that we could feed it straight into the program. She happily accepted my offer and went off to bed.

I duly arrived on the day and she greeted me with coffee and cake, which most people know I have a weakness for. After some chit-chat and catching up with the newly arrived son and the beagle, we got to work. She had been very thorough in having all the necessary paperwork to hand because of organising the finances for the car. In fact, she knew her household expenses pretty well.

Now I am not disclosing her name for privacy reasons, but I know she would have no issue in presenting her story and the numbers. Even those I am not going to go into in depth. But there are things that sometimes leave financial advisers totally blown away. The stories we hear about what people are doing with their money would leave most astonished and flabbergasted. Just when you hear one story that is unbelievable, someone has an even better one!

And so it was with a few items that appeared in the household spending. Suffice it to say, she was given a well-needed financial education on the day. However, the more important thing was not what I said, but the results from the program. So we finished putting in all the numbers for the first time around and looked at the results in advance. You have actually seen them already on a previous page.

They had total debts of $353,333 over 30 years. The interest was $265,122. Now when you look at the left-hand column, the interest could be reduced to $169,357 and down to 21 years. That's a saving of $95,765 and nearly 9 years. Keep in mind, we didn't change anything. Same expenses, same income.

No changes at all. It's not what they are doing, but how they are doing it!

Here's that summary again.

Results In Advance

	Current	Money Rules
Total Debts	353.333	353.333
Total Interest	265.122.74	169.357.39
Years	30	21.08

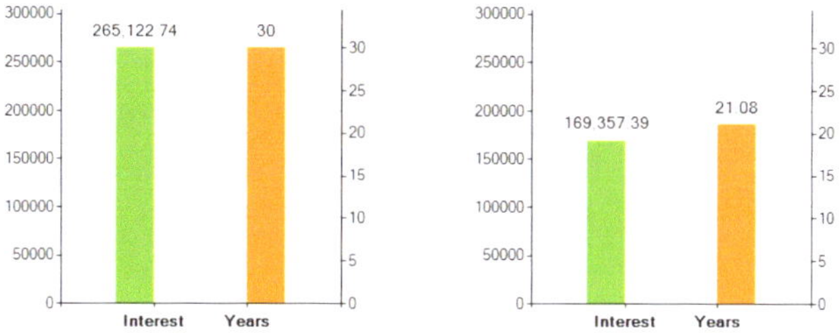

	Current	Money Rules
Interest Saved	0	95.765.35
Years Saved	0	8.92
Debt Free	Mar. 2051	Mar. 2042

We did some tweaking just with her expenses and a few other little adjustments. I say little, but the program proves just how powerful small changes can be. I don't always like to share these results, because people start to make silly comparisons thinking they could then get similar results.

It is important to understand that no two people will *ever* get the same results for a number of reasons. Too many to go into here, but even twins will never get the same results.

So here is the revised Results In Advance report. The left-hand column remains the same because that's the starting point. Now have a look at the right-hand column to see the differences.

The interest payments have been reduced to $88,652 and the term is down to 11 years. That's a saving of $176,470 wasted interest and nearly 19 years in lost time.

Results In Advance

	Current	Money Rules
Total Debts	353,333	353,333
Total Interest	265,122.74	88,652.02
Years	30	11.08

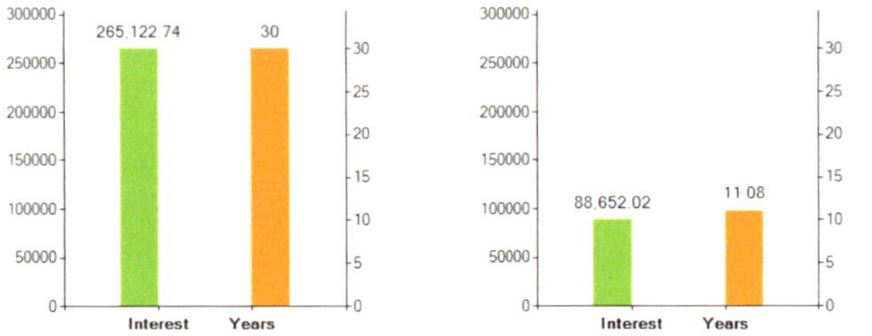

	Current	Money Rules
Interest Saved	0	176,470.72
Years Saved	0	18.92
Debt Free	Mar. 2051	Mar. 2032

Needless to say, she was amazed with the results and the look of relief on her face was reward enough, together with the cake of course

But the story didn't end there. Now that she could see her financial future mapped out in such a simple format, she was already starting to work out how she could make it better. For instance, her husband was due for a promotion at his work in a few months time and the increase in salary would be a further $20,000. So we put that into the program as a scenario and it made a huge difference.

I left her place that day knowing I had brought some light into a dark space, and she was now filled with a fresh perspective for her future with new hope, dreams and goals. She rang me two weeks later to tell me all the companies she had been in touch with and the money she had saved after negotiating with them.

I told her to be greedy with her money, and it started resonating with her. It shouldn't just be given away to everyone or every company just because they say that's the way that it is. Challenge them to do better or you'll take your business to someone who will.

Life changes. The family sold that home and moved interstate. She now enjoys a really well paid job. She also knows she can just dive back into her Money Rules account at any time to update the numbers and set a new financial course for tomorrow and beyond.

There's more to the story than that. We also mapped out how much money they would have available at retirement. That was before I created the retirement module in 2017 which goes even further in setting them up for a financially secure future.

The initial program showed anyone how to manage their money and eliminate debt faster, as you've already seen. The Lifestyle module takes the money that is saved and shows how much will be needed to live on in retirement. No more waiting until you get there to find out how much you'll need. I can guarantee you that for most people, their money is going to run out of life before they do. Too little too late by then!

This means living a life dependent on social security and likely in poverty. Ask a person living on a pension what it's like and I'll guarantee you they will say they wished they started doing more, sooner. When I asked why they didn't, they told me they were too busy paying bills. And this is where people go wrong.

Have you seen how much debt the governments have been racking up?

Who do you think is going to pay for that? You, your kids, your grandchildren and great-grandchildren and probably even their kids. The social security pot will run out one day, and there won't be anything left to pay pensioners or the needy.

You have to do it for yourself, because, no-one else is going to do it for you.

Imagine standing on a sinking ship in the middle of the ocean on a very dark night. No one knows where you are, and there's no one coming to save you!

Don't spend 40 years working to end up living 20, 30, or 40 years in poverty. You need to start sooner rather than later. You need to start right now. Get good advice, and be committed. You only get one chance on this merry-go-round so you may as well make it a good one.

Can you achieve the same results as the example above? I don't know!

One thing I am certain of is that you can do better than what you are currently.

Whether you do it with Money Rules or without, do it for yourself and your future lifestyle.

You can get the Results In Advance report. Go to moneyrules.com.au/ria

MONEY RULES - THE AUTHOR EXPERTISE

Reflecting on my years as a financial advisor, I can't help but recognize that the very steps I advocate in Money Rules mirror my own financial transformation.

However, it's worth noting that when I embarked on this journey, I had no guiding hand or roadmap. It was a journey fueled by instinct, starting slowly and then gaining momentum, ultimately shredding and shedding debts and accumulating financial resources for the things I'd tirelessly worked for throughout my life.

My personal commitments included mortgages on both my home and office, car leases, office and business operational expenses, and the added responsibility of managing my colleague's extensive portfolio of clients which I had acquired after his retirement.

Moreover, I bore the sole responsibility of generating income to cover the financial obligations, including the substantial wages of five well-paid staff members. Despite the weight of these overheads, I found daily motivation not only in meeting these financial commitments but also in the profound fulfilment of helping and guiding clients toward their financial futures.

During this period, I developed a keen interest in the financial aspects of the business. I began meticulously tracking all previous incomes and expenses, mapping the sources and destinations of our earnings. This meticulous approach provided me with a clear action plan, enabling me to concentrate on activities that were most income-generating while streamlining those that didn't contribute significantly. Having a deep understanding of our financials offered valuable insights into growing the business efficiently and effectively.

It almost felt like a financial miracle had swept into my life, systematically cleaning up my financial landscape. Each day became more exciting as I chipped away at various financial obligations. Over time, I stood debt-free, with all my income entirely my own.

This transformation didn't happen overnight, and it was through this process that I realized the true power of effective money management and decided to create the Money Rules program to share this knowledge with others.

Life takes on a whole new meaning when financial burdens, such as mortgages and looming payments, are eliminated. The knowledge that your bank account holds more than enough to plan a vacation or even a spontaneous weekend getaway transforms life into a less stressful and more enjoyable experience.

Empowered by my financial transformation, I eagerly shared this newfound wisdom with my clients, who were immensely grateful. Yet, it wasn't until a few years after I'd sold my financial planning practice in 2006 that the idea of creating the Money Rules program even crossed my mind.

In 2008, after two years of globetrotting to global destinations and embarking on epic four-wheel drive adventures across Australia's vast landscapes, I found myself standing in my front yard, surveying the completed landscaping and renovations to our home. Everything was done, and the sense of accomplishment was satisfying.

However, under the warm sun's embrace, it struck me like a bolt of inspiration - I was feeling unfulfilled. It seemed like a switch went off inside my head. I still had the urge to help people with managing their finances, but I wanted to do it differently, outside the confines of the regulated financial world governed by banks and insurance companies. The one recurring question my clients had always posed was how to manage their day-to-day finances.

They'd say,' I don't want insurance, investment or retirement advice. I just want to know, "How do I manage my daily money?"

The rising cost of living and stagnant wages had placed many in a precarious situation. They were tasked with doing more with less, and when they ran out of cash, credit cards became their lifeline for basic necessities. Yet, when the credit card bills arrived, they could only afford to pay the minimum, trapping themselves in a vicious cycle of mounting debt.

They were desperate for guidance and looked to me for help as their financial advisor.

If I had my time all over again, my most pressing goal would be to get my clients debt-free far more quickly and on the road to prosperity. We didn't have the tools available to us back then as we do today.

In my quest to find a program that aligned with my vision, I explored various avenues and even invested $27,000 with a Western Australian company, only to discover that it primarily focused on debt refinancing and expense management—a strategy that didn't resonate with my philosophy.

Unable to find a suitable solution, I embarked on the journey to create my own. Admittedly, I wasn't a tech wizard or a computer programmer, but my determination led me to search for a way to craft a program that met my exacting requirements. The program's ultimate goal was to empower individuals to manage their finances effectively without the need for refinancing, remortgaging, or resorting to desperate measures.

My best ideas often came to mind while washing the cars, working in the garden, cutting the grass, or taking long walks. One morning, as I stood in the shower, it all clicked into place. I spent the next two weeks writing out how the program should work and diligently jotted down every thought to create this program. To my surprise, when I handed it over to the programmers for implementation, they expressed delight at the level of detail I'd provided, describing precisely what needed to be built. It was remarkably accurate.

Since its inception, the program has undergone minor adjustments. The only significant addition was in the form of a retirement planning module. Money Rules was initially conceived just to help manage money, but it turned into a debt elimination machine. It took me a few years to realize it could also cater to those seeking financial certainty during retirement, which has since become an essential aspect of our financial journey.

The reality is that many individuals are at risk of retiring in poverty due to inadequate financial preparations during their working years. With governments struggling to sustain aging pension schemes and numerous retirement funds faltering due to poor investments, the need for financial empowerment for individuals is greater than ever.

Today, Money Rules stands as a comprehensive program offering detailed information and a personalized blueprint for anyone with the means to create a tailored plan that aligns with their unique needs.

Recognizing that not everyone desires the full-fledged Money Rules program, the Fast Track meeting was introduced to provide individuals with financial consulting and guidance. Once the Fast Track meeting is complete, you are free to implement the strategies and solutions.

For those seeking continuous access and convenience, we offer the digital software version of Money Rules designed to complement the comprehensive planning accomplished during the Fast Track meeting.

Allow me to address a concern that might be going on in your head and others have previously raised. Why does Money Rules cost as much as it does when there are so many other much cheaper options available?

A few immediate answers are these:

- If current options worked, then there would be no need for Money Rules
- When you pay $47 or $97 you get $47 or $97 solutions
- What most people offer are the same old budgets - they work, people don't
- You get what you pay for
- You get to work with a professional and a system, not budgets
- You have a choice between budgets, advisers, coaches or Money Rules
- Most options just manage your money, Money Rules creates your future
- You'll know if it's the right fit for you by the end of the Fast Track session

Either you create your future, or live one designed for you.

If you choose to extend your investment in the program after your Fast Track experience, transitioning to the software version is the natural progression in your financial journey. The return on investment in the software exceeds its cost. Upon completing the Fast Track, you'll truly appreciate its value.

With the Money Rules program, you'll enjoy 24/7 access from anywhere with an internet connection.

This comprehensive program grants you access to both the debt elimination and retirement planning components, empowering you to take control of your financial journey.

When you invest in Money Rules, you essentially have your personalised financial plan and money management tool at your fingertips. You can effortlessly make updates or adjustments whenever it suits you or when your circumstances change.

You are not left alone to set up a program without any idea of why certain numbers are entered into a certain category or how to select and implement the best strategies. This is a done with you service from the beginning and our priority is your complete satisfaction so that you clearly understand every aspect of the program and the results and how they impact on your life before you invest.

Your Move

Now, I entrust this opportunity to you and eagerly anticipate our meeting when you decide to embark on a transformative journey in your financial life.

If you're inclined to go deeper into this journey, I encourage you to take that initial step by obtaining the Results In Advance report. That's where it all begins. It will illuminate your current financial position and reveal the potential awaiting you.

Remember the story at the beginning, the one about 'Acres Of Diamonds,' where the riches were right beneath the farmer's feet.

If only he had known?

This tale resonates with many of us. We work diligently for our money, yet the outcomes may not always be obvious or match our expectations. It's possible that hidden treasures are already within your reach, just waiting to be uncovered.

It could be said that the grass on the other side of the fence was only greener because it had been watered. All that may be needed is nurturing your own grass!

Imagine this is the key to your future. It's your shortcut to success.

“The secret to wealth is not how much you make, but how much you keep!”

- Nobby Kleinman

ABOUT THE AUTHOR

A Glimpse into the Author's Financial Experience

Allow me to introduce myself. I'm Nobby Kleinman, an ex financial adviser with over two decades of experience in the regulated world of money and financial planning. Throughout my career, I have had the privilege of working with more than 4,000 clients, including individuals, employers, employees, and CEOs. My journey has been a tapestry of financial stories, and each one has shaped my perspective on the importance of financial independence.

My expertise extends beyond numbers and spreadsheets. I've witnessed firsthand the challenges that women face when it comes to their financial well-being, from life-altering events like divorce and widowhood to the need for empowerment and control. It's these experiences that have fueled my passion to help others navigate their financial journeys.

The same challenges apply to men in their roles as single fathers raising children or perhaps even adjusting to a new lifestyle after life's challenges. I've been to the funerals of wonderful clients and even friends. I've had the privilege to deliver insurance claims cheques to grieving families and have been touched by the sadness of death and despair about their futures about how and where to start.

In my role as a financial advisor, I've had the privilege of guiding individuals and couples towards financial security and independence. The lessons I've learned, the success stories I've witnessed, and the transformations I've been a part of have all culminated in the creation of Money Rules—an intelligent financial system designed to empower you on your path to financial freedom.

Throughout this book, you'll find my genuine desire to make a positive impact on your financial life. My goal is to share the knowledge, insights, and tools that can help you take control of your financial destiny. Together, we'll embark on a journey towards a brighter and more secure financial future.

The Inspiration Behind Money Rules

The inspiration behind Money Rules is rooted in a deep understanding of the challenges individuals face on their financial journeys. It was born out of the recognition that traditional financial approaches often fall short of providing true financial independence. Most are there to sell financial products or investments.

Today, many are sold by opportunistic people calling themselves money coaches who hide behind a thin veneer of financial achievements, posing as experts and having an attitude of faking it until they make it. And then they just disappear or end up in court.

There are two types of money coaches, real ones and opportunistic ones. People who are actually qualified with a broad range of financial experience and those who are in for the quick buck. They thought it might be a good idea to be a money coach. Their goal is to book as many months as possible with appointments and generate ongoing income. These people are often only one step ahead of those they coach.

Money Rules works differently. It goes directly to the core of your financials right at the very beginning and devises your individual lifetime strategy from day one with a push-button solution. It answers the question those women asked me.

My motivation to create Money Rules came from witnessing the real struggles that women and families experienced due to inadequate financial planning and support.

I wanted to create a system that would empower individuals to overcome these challenges and achieve lasting financial security.

The idea was to develop a financial tool that would be more than just a budgeting app or investment platform. Money Rules was designed to be a comprehensive system that addresses the unique financial needs and goals of individuals, offering practical solutions for every step of their financial journey.

As you read this book and explore the world of Money Rules, you'll gain insight into the vision and inspiration behind this transformative financial system. It's my hope that you'll find it as empowering and life-changing as I intended it to be.

I'm not just an author, although I have written a number of books and many articles. I am someone who is deeply passionate about helping individuals like you achieve financial freedom. I believe that meaningful connections are the foundation of effective financial guidance.

If you ever have questions or simply want to share your financial journey, you can reach out through Money Rules.com.au so that I can assist you on your path to financial independence.

If what Money Rules can do for you piques your interest, then at least find out how it can change your life. I'll say again, that to get started there is currently no cost because I want to make it as easy as I can to extend at least some light into the darkness and shadows that cast fear and uncertainty into the hearts of people who think they have no hope.

My premise is that there is always another way.

Don't tell me it can't be done.

Show me how it can!

That's what I want for you.

Let Money Rules show you what's possible!

I'm excited to embark on this journey with you, and I look forward to being a part of your transformation towards a life of financial abundance and independence.

Together, we can make your financial dreams a reality.

Nobby Kleinman
MONEY RULES

Dip. Adv FS (FP) - BGB

Made in the USA
Monee, IL
05 November 2026

67385919R00062